LEVEL
2

Storms

Miriam Busch Goin

NATIONAL
GEOGRAPHIC

Washington, D.C.

To S.R. and N.J. – forces of nature, both. – M.B.G.

Copyright © 2009 National Geographic Society.
This British English edition published in 2017 by Collins, An imprint of HarperCollins*Publishers*,
The News Building, 1 London Bridge Street, London. SE1 9GF.

Browse the complete Collins catalogue at
www.collins.co.uk

A catalogue record for this publication is available from the British Library.

ISBN: 978-0-00-826662-2
US Edition ISBN: 978-1-4263-1577-0

COVER, 26-27 bottom: © Visuals Unlimited/ Corbis; 1: © Pekka Parviainen/ Photo Researchers, Inc.; 2: © David
Epperson/ Stone/ Getty Images; 4: © Roy Corral/ Stone/ Getty Images; 4-5: © Phil Degginger/ Alamy; 5: © Danny
Lehman/ Corbis; 6-7, 32 top left: © Roine Magnusson/ Stone/ Getty Images; 8-9, 32 bottom left: © Jhaz Photography/
Shutterstock; 10 left, 10-11, 14-15, 32 bottom right: © Gene Rhoden/ Weatherpix Stock Images; 12 top: © IntraClique/
Shutterstock; 12-13: © Sebastian Knight/ Shutterstock; 13 right: © Jim Reed/Photo Researchers RM/Getty Images; 16-17:
© Ingo Arndt/ Minden Pictures/ NationalGeographicStock.com; 18-19: © Hiroyuki Matsumoto/ Photographer's Choice/
Getty Images; 20-21: © Steve McCurry/ NationalGeographicStock.com; 22-23: © Mike Hill/ Alamy; 24-25: © NASA/JPL/SSI;
26-27 top: © Anatoli Styf/ Shutterstock; 27 top: © Kazuyoshi Nomachi/ Corbis; 27 bottom, 32 top right: © Solvin Zankl/
Photographer's Choice/ Getty Images; 28: © JTB Photo Communications, Inc./ Alamy; 29 top: © Alvaro Leiva/
Photolibrary.com; 29 bottom: © Science Faction/ Getty Images; 30: © Norbert Rosing/ National Geographic/
Getty Images; 31 top: © Gustavo Fadel/ Shutterstock; 31 bottom: © Jaipal Singh/ epa/ Corbis.

Printed and bound in China by RR Donnelley APS

MIX
Paper from
responsible sources

FSC
www.fsc.org
FSC™ C007454

This book is produced from independently certified FSC™ paper
to ensure responsible forest management.

For more information visit: www.harpercollins.co.uk/green

Table of Contents

Weather!

Storms are important.
Living things need fresh water
from rain and snow

Wind can help clean the air.
Weather cools and heats our
planet so it is just right for life.

Clouds are made of drops
of water so small that
they float.

These clouds look heavy and grey.
Can you hear the wind blow?
Leaves wave back and forth on
branches. What's happening?
Wild, wonderful, stormy weather!

Weather Words

Weather:
What it is
like outside.

Thunder and Lightning

Flash! Boom!

In these storm clouds, the drops of water have frozen. Little ice crystals are bumping wildly against big crystals. This makes lightning. Lightning heats the air quickly. This very fast temperature change makes sound waves. The sound is thunder!

Weather Words

Crystal: A shape that is the same on many sides.

Lightning is electricity.
It is hotter than the sun.
Some lightning jumps from
cloud to cloud. Some jumps
from the ground to the sky.

Lightning can make loops and
patterns in the sky. It can even roll
in a ball. Lightning bolts can travel
95km or more.

Weather Words

Electricity: Energy that can be natural or man-made.

This is ribbon lightning. It happens when strong winds push the lightning bolts sideways.

Hailstorm

Thunk! Clunk!
Some thunderstorms make
hailstones. Hailstones are not
stones. They are ice.

Ice crystals in some thunderclouds get tumbled in the cloud. They get bigger and bigger until they are so heavy they fall. Hail can be big or small. It can be round or long.

These are unusually big hailstones!

Tornado

Strong winds blow.
Dark clouds cover the sky.
Hail falls. Suddenly, it is quiet.
In the distance, a cone-shaped
funnel cloud touches the ground.
Tornado! Twister! Cyclone!
These are all names for a fierce,
fast, twisting wind.

Over water, tornadoes are called
"waterspouts".

Weather Words

Funnel:
A cone shape that is wider at the top.

Sandstorm

A wall of wind picks up sand.
As the wind crosses the land,
it picks up more sand. The
wall grows higher.

When it roars past, it can knock down fences. In Australia, they call the storms willy-willys. In Sudan, they call them haboobs.

Blizzard

Snowflakes fall from very cold clouds. A cold wind blows the snow so hard you cannot see in front of you.

Snowflakes are ice crystals. In a blizzard there are billions and trillions of snowflakes.

Monsoon

Monsoons are winds that change each season. India has only two seasons. Winter monsoons are dry.

Summer monsoons bring LOTS of rain. Everyone cheers because the rains help food grow.

Hurricane

It is late summer. Dark clouds form over the ocean. Strong winds pull ocean water up into spinning clouds. Hurricane! Cyclone! Typhoon! Hurricane winds knock down houses. Water floods streets and homes. Hurricane winds spin in a circle. The middle of a hurricane is still and calm. It is called the "eye" of the storm.

Out of this World!

Where are the worst storms?
Not on Earth!

Jupiter's hurricane has been
blowing for more than 400
years! In 2006, a lightning storm
on Saturn lasted for weeks. The
lightning bolts were more than
1,000 times stronger than Earth's!
Neptune has winds that blow
1,450km per hour!

Jupiter's hurricane is called the Great Red Spot.

Guess!

Storms are made of many
small parts. Together with wind,
these tiny bits are strong!
Guess what each tiny bit is.

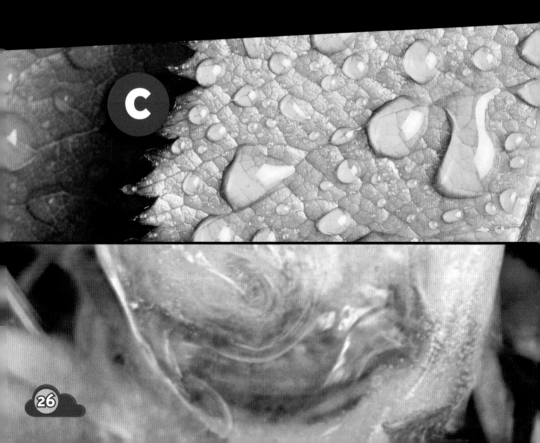

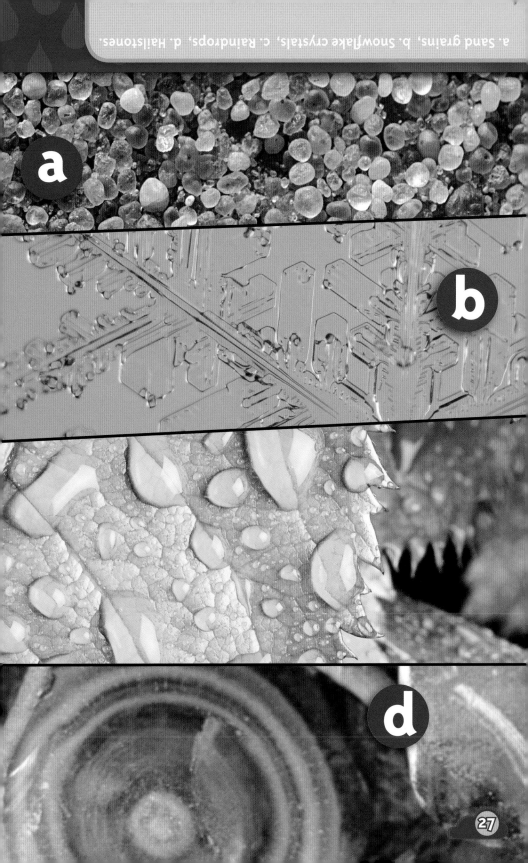

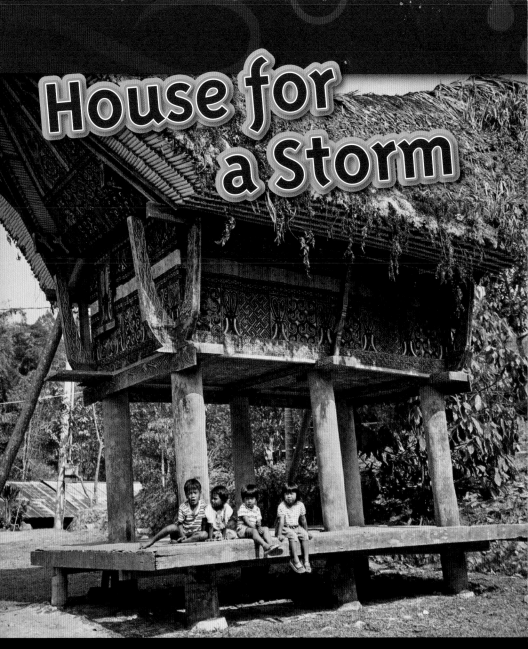

House for a Storm

This home is on stilts. After a monsoon, water and mud flow under the house.

In a sandstorm this tent keeps sand out. An underground storm cellar keeps people safe during a tornado.

Wild Animals, Wild Weather

In blizzard winds these muskoxen huddle together. They face the wind so their bodies stay warmer.

In a haboob, camels shut a second pair of eyelids to protect their eyes from sand. Their long, thin nostrils and extra-hairy ears keep sand out.

In monsoon rains, some monkeys keep dry in buildings or under branches. Other monkeys don't mind getting wet.

WEATHER
What it is like outside.

CRYSTAL
A shape that is the same on many sides.

ELECTRICITY
Energy that can be natural or man-made.

FUNNEL
A cone shape that is wider at the top.